WildAboutYou

LEADER'S GUIDE

LifeWay Press®
Nashville, Tennessee

© 2006 LifeWay Press®
Reprinted February 2006

No part of this work may be reproduced or transmitted in any form or by any means,
electronic or mechanical, including photocopying and recording, or by any information
storage or retrieval system, except as may be expressly permitted in writing by the
publisher. Requests for permission should be addressed in writing to LifeWay Press®,
One LifeWay Plaza, Nashville, TN 37234-0174.

ISBN: 1-4158-2918-7

Dewey Decimal Classification Number: 248.83
Subject Heading: TEENAGERS \ CHRISTIAN LIFE \ GIRLS

Printed in the United States of America

Student Ministry Publishing
LifeWay Church Resources
One LifeWay Plaza
Nashville, Tennessee 37234-0174

We believe the Bible has God for its author; salvation for its end; and truth, without any
mixture of error, for its matter and that all Scripture is totally true and trustworthy.
The 2000 statement of *The Baptist Faith and Message* is our doctrinal guideline.

Unless otherwise indicated, all Scripture quotations are taken from the *Holman Christian
Standard Bible*® Copyright © 1999, 2000, 2002, 2003 by Holman Bible Publishers.
Used by permission. *Holman Christian Standard Bible*®, Holman CSB®, and HCSB®
are federally registered trademarks of Holman Bible Publishers.

Scripture quotations marked *(THE MESSAGE)* are taken from *THE MESSAGE*. Copyright ©
by Eugene Peterson, 1993, 1994, 1995. Used by permission of NavPress Publishing Group.

Scripture quotations marked (NIV) are taken from the *Holy Bible, New International
Version,* copyright © 1973, 1978, 1984 by International Bible Society.

Derived from the book, *Do You Think I'm Beautiful?*, copyright © 2003 by Angela Thomas
and published with the agreement of Thomas Nelson Publishers.

Published in association with Creative Trust, Inc., 2105 Elliston Place, Nashville, TN 37203.
For more information about Angela Thomas, e-mail info@creativetrust.com or visit
www.angelathomas.com.

LEADER'S GUIDE

A Powerful Study at Hand

INSIDE THE HEART OF EVERY WOMAN lies a question that begs to be answered: Do you think I'm beautiful?

Women of all ages and from all backgrounds ask this question. Middle-age physicists. Retired teachers. Beautiful queens. Wives of long-haul truck drivers. Foreign ambassadors. Brilliant professors. A woman suffering from Multiple Sclerosis. This question lies at the core of a woman's heart—even in the heart of teenage girls.

Just look at our cultural landscape for evidence of this heart cry. Can't you see the teen girls screaming out for an answer? Some scream through their clothes—or the lack of them. Some cry out by abusing their bodies with alcohol, drugs, or even razors. Many trade their purity for approval from a guy. Others have already answered the question for themselves and just fade into the background, certain that their worst fear is true: they don't matter.

A Critical Lesson

Angela Thomas, best-selling author of the book *Do You Think I'm Beautiful?* upon which this study is based, states the importance of girls learning the lesson of God's untamable love early in their lives. In the DVD accompanying this study, you'll hear Angela say something like this: "The Enemy is out to take teens out early. He is out to destroy every person, but it's as if teen girls have a big target on their backs, outlined in neon lights. If he can hurt teen girls early, they will fall prey to the Enemy and limp into adulthood wounded. It's critical for teen girls to grasp that God is truly wild about them, that He calls them beautiful, and that He wants an intimate, passionate relationship

with them unlike anything they've ever known."

If teenage girls can begin to grasp the concept that their self-worth lies in the unchangeable, uncontainable love of God, then they can build their lives on a rock-solid foundation that cannot be shaken by their body size, their mistakes, or the opinions of others. They can live in confidence instead of insecurity, trust instead of fear, hope instead of cynicism and reservation.

Unfortunately, countless young women have not heard that God is wild about them. They have bought into the lie that they're not tall enough, smart enough, funny enough, or skinny enough. Culture has baited an unattainable goal of perfection through outward appearance and performance, and teen girls have swallowed that bait—hook, line, and sinker.

The Road Ahead

The fact that you have picked up this book bears witness that your own soul has asked this question and you desire for teen girls to learn this answer. Chances are, you need to hear the truths of this study as much as the students do. All women need to be reminded of their place in the Father's arms as His beloved. As you lead, feel the freedom to be honest with the girls about your own struggles (as appropriate, without it becoming all about you). It's OK to share how you've been wounded or which lies of the Enemy tend to trip you up. Girls will relate better to authenticity than to a plastic faith that has not been tested by the fires of trial. Over the course of the next six weeks, you all will experience the uncontainable love of God and will begin to live in the reality that God is wild about you!✲

Leading *Wild About You*

CONGRATULATIONS! You've decided to embark on an amazing adventure by leading a girls' Bible study. As you think about the weeks ahead, you may have some questions.

Who Should Be a Part of This Study?

This study is designed for teen girls, grades 7-12. However, many youth groups incorporate sixth grade students in their ministries. While some of these preteen girls may grasp the contents in this study easily, many may struggle with some of the concepts. If you involve sixth grade girls, consider going at a slower pace or altering significantly the teaching plans for these concrete thinkers.

This study deals with questions in every girl's heart, so you can involve both Christians and non-Christians. In fact, this study could be a great outreach study for girls who need to know about a God who loves them deeply.

How Large Should the Groups Be?

To create the best possible environment for discussion, openness, and vulnerability, try to keep the groups to 10 girls or less. If you have more girls who want to do this study, form more than one group. You may want to form groups based on age or school grade. This would provide groups of similar maturity and cognitive levels.

You also may want to form groups of girls of various ages. This would allow older girls to be examples and mentors to younger girls. One church in California involved college students in the study, hoping to pair these older students with younger ones later in a mentoring program.

This study allowed leaders to see how the girls naturally "clicked" with the collegiates.

If you want to build unity among all the girls doing the study, you may want to have all of the groups meet together once a month or meet for part of the time together. You could do an opening activity together or watch the video together. However, having all of the groups meet at the same time limits the location of the study. Consider which is more important for you.

Where Should This Study Take Place?

This Bible study can take place in a church, but that's probably the last place you'll want to consider. As a better alternative, host the study at someone's home. This relaxed atmosphere will lend itself more to open dialogue. Tear away the barriers of being at church and the "Sunday School answers" that come with that setting. When choosing a home to host, consider the space you'll need based on the number of girls who have signed up. You'll need a comfortable place that has a DVD player and TV.

Because you're meeting in a non-traditional setting, keep in mind that the resources you'd have at the church may not be at your fingertips. Give yourself plenty of time to gather necessary supplies.

What Will I Need?

Every girl will need a student book (looks like a magazine), a Bible, and a pen that will write well in the student book. (Test several pens to see which work the best). The supplies and resources you'll need for each week's study are listed at the beginning of the teaching plan. These supplies will vary from week to week.✻

Jazz It Up: Creative Tips and Extras

IN THIS STUDY, girls will learn how God views them as unique, beautiful, and the objects of His pursuit. Foster this understanding by making the study unique, too. Check out these ideas to add a special touch.

Introducing the Study

Getting the word out about the study is important. Use these creative ideas to generate interest and excitement.

Invitations. Create buzz about the study by sending out special invitations. Since this study focuses on God's passionate love, you may even want your invitations to look like wedding announcements. Send these to girls in advance and follow up with phone calls, e-mails, and so forth.

Let's party. To kick off the study, host a party. You may want to do an elaborate party, complete with decorations, a meal, and an introduction to the study. If you want to make it less formal, invite girls over to watch a movie like "The Princess Diaries" that mirrors the theme in this study: you are beautiful even though you may not realize it. Let girls pitch in for pizza and drinks.

Church-wide launch. Coordinate with the women's ministry in your church to launch the study for women and teens at the same time. The adult women can study *Do You Think I'm Beautiful? Bible Study and Journal* (Thomas Nelson Publishers, ISBN 0-7852-6223-7) while the teen girls study *Wild About You.* Host a church-wide women's event (like a tea party) to launch the study.

Gifts to Give

To make this Bible study memorable for the girls, consider giving them special gifts in conjunction with the study.

Special pens. Girls love unique pens that write in different colors, including metallic. Check out craft stores (in the scrapbooking section) for different kinds of pens. Some department stores package several colors together and sell them with the school supplies. Make sure that the ink doesn't smear in the books.

Journals. Some girls like to journal; others don't. If you know the personality of the group you'll be leading, you can determine if a journal would be an appropriate and appreciated gift. Wholesale retail stores sometimes offer bundles of journals, so you might want to check there for a good deal.

Bracelets/necklaces. Girls love jewelry! Find an inexpensive bracelet or necklace with a charm that could symbolize the truths of this study. At the end of the study (or at the closing celebration described below), present these as a spiritual marker and memory.

A Retreat Alternative

As an alternative to a weekly study, you can use this material in a retreat format. Begin on Friday evening with the opening session. Continue through Saturday and end on Sunday morning, if possible. Build in lots of girl-time: facials, beauty tips, movies, panel discussions, and so forth. If possible, end the weekend with a closing celebration that involves their family and the church.

Closing Celebration

To end the study, plan a closing celebration in which girls are blessed and affirmed by their family (especially their fathers) and the church body. For more information on this idea, see pages 31-32. ❋

Girls' Ministry in the Church

By J. Merritt Johnston

SARAH WAS ONE OF THOSE GIRLS who appeared to have it all together. Her peers looked up to her and the youth leaders respected her. But she had a secret that she would never dare to share.

Although she tried to champion the concept of godly beauty to the girls in the youth group, she was secretly suffering with an eating disorder. The disease that was eating away her body was eating away her soul as well. Fear of what others might think consumed her, so Sarah remained silent in her struggle.

That was Sarah's unshared story when I met her three years ago. I was speaking at a SAGE Girls' Conference when she approached me after one of the sessions. With tears streaming down her face, she shared her secret.

Today Sarah is a thriving college student at a small, Christian school. I believe the success of her life today stems from that moment three years ago when she began to break free from the stronghold in her life.

Six years ago God planted a vision in the hearts of 12 college students. The vision was built around the idea of influencing and equipping young women to be radicals for the cause of Christ.

I was blessed to be one of those 12 students, and I've been part of the incredible journey to pursue that God-given vision ever since. What began as a small community Bible study has now grown into SAGE Ministries, a nationally known organization that offers everything from conferences to curriculum.

Although the efforts of SAGE Ministries hopefully have served to impact young women in a profound way, I am certain that the hope for these girls is found in the hands and hearts of God's church.

Over the last six years, we have seen God explode the vision of girls' ministry in the hearts of moms, ministers, and everyone in between. We believe God is raising up His church to reach out to His girls, and we are excited about partnering with the local church in that process.

As part of that partnership, we have made it a priority to offer seminars for the sponsors who attend our conferences. In these sessions, I try to communicate the value of four things:

1. Harnessing Your Passion

Passion is often hard to find in a society that is raising a generation too apathetic to vote in the presidential race but aggressive enough to cast two million votes in the last American Idol contest.

Our society has a skewed perspective on what really matters, and the effects have trickled down to our teenagers. We are facing an uphill battle because there is a godly minority trying to overcome a worldly majority. In many ways, the church is failing and the fallout ranges from sexual promiscuity to suicide attempts.

Passion is the only thing to set you apart from the programmed apathy that has become so prevalent. Girls are sensitive, and they can sense when someone is serving out of passion rather than obligation. Take your passion to reach girls for Christ and share that with others. You'll find that passion is contagious. God has given other people the same heart, and many are just looking for a passionate leader to follow.

2. Outlining Your Purpose

Many of the ministry teams I have spoken with are not failing for lack of passion. They are failing for lack of purpose. Passion without purpose is as useless as talk without action, yet many teams never take the time to define their purpose before making a plan.

You and your team need to add some arms and legs to the heart of your ministry by outlining its purpose. Ask yourself questions like …

- What is the ultimate goal of our ministry?
- What do we want girls to gain from this ministry?

After asking ourselves similar questions, our team settled on this purpose statement: *To reach, teach, and train young women to impact their communities and the world.*

This statement reflects our desire to see three things accomplished in our ministry.

a. To reach girls (Evangelism)—We carry the hope of the world in our hearts, and it's imperative that we reach out to others with the truth of the gospel. Girls' ministries have to be more than just a haven for those who are already heaven-bound. They have to be beacons to those who have never seen the light of Christ.

b. To teach girls (Discipleship)— Matthew 28:19-20 calls us to make disciples, not just converts. Beyond reaching girls with the gospel, we have to teach girls what it looks like to be godly.

c. To train girls (Equipping)—No one is more uniquely gifted to minister to girls than other girls. We want to seize the opportunity to show them how to leverage their spiritual gifts and abilities for the cause of Christ.

This purpose statement reflects our vision in a clear and concise way. It steers us away from distractions that would hinder our purpose and keeps us focused on the task at hand. Take the time to develop a purpose statement that will help you do the same.

3. Developing Your Philosophy

A purpose outlines what you hope to accomplish but often is fuzzy on how you plan to do so. I believe this is why developing a ministry philosophy is so vital.

As our team began traveling, we realized how important it was for us to develop a ministry philosophy for our conferences. We wanted guidelines to assist us in the planning process as we evaluated everything from teaching methods to stage setup. Our time at each stop was limited, so we wanted to make the most of each moment we had with these students.

At a planning retreat, we prayerfully poured over our philosophy. We prayed. We debated. We added. We deleted. Then we agreed on the following words: *personal, biblical,* and *relevant*. These three concepts became our ministry's core values.

a. Personal. Girls want people to be real, so we decided to let it all hang out. Sharing our personal testimonies became a central piece of our conference puzzle. We wanted the girls to know we've been there, done that, and made it through with God's help. Beyond that, we intentionally programmed our conferences to include break-out sessions where they could meet us face-to-face. We wanted to be both genuine and accessible, and we discovered that girls overwhelmingly respond to this approach.

b. Biblical. Matthew 7:6 says, *"Don't reduce holy mysteries to slogans"* (THE MESSAGE). We realized we had a tendency to sugarcoat the Word of God instead of speaking the truth in love. Our messages were built around stories meant to make them laugh rather than Scripture meant to make them think. We had to make a fresh commitment to open girls' eyes to the glory of God by sharing the power of His Word.

When we start teaching about God's sovereignty more than our sin, I believe we succeed in treating the disease rather than just the symptoms. As girls grow in their knowledge of God, they also grow in their sensitivity to the Holy Spirit. They are motivated to honor God in issues of modesty and purity out of love rather than fear or guilt. I've witnessed this firsthand, and it's amazing to watch girls change radically from the inside out.

c. Relevant. Some people sacrifice biblical integrity for the sake of "being relevant," but I believe it's possible for the two to coexist. As long as you're teaching God's Word, you're free to be as creative as you want. We're not entertainers, nor should we feel the pressure to be. But Jesus Himself taught in a manner that was both biblical and engaging. We should be able to do the same. Not only should our teaching style be relevant, but our topics must be also. We have to stop tiptoeing around the tough issues. Girls are battling poor self-images bred in a society that demands physical perfection by whatever means necessary. The fruits of these demands are eating disorders, self-mutilation, and even plastic surgery. We are committed to tackle issues such as sex, immodesty, and self-image in a candid, no-holds-barred way, and the girls respect us for our honesty. They'll respect yours as well.

We found that partnering our purpose with our philosophy unified our team and aligned our direction. Whenever we faced a decision, we could evaluate the idea with our purpose and our philosophy in mind. Your core values might be completely different from what we chose, but I guarantee

you'll experience the same benefits by having a philosophy to follow.

4. Implementing a Plan

Once you've done all the preparation, it's time to take action. But before you put any event on the calendar …

- Evaluate people's passions. If someone has a heart for girls, get to know that person and plug her in appropriately.
- Review your purpose with your team and develop strategies that will accomplish it. Put a copy of your purpose in a prominent place so you have it as a reference for long-range planning.
- Examine your philosophy and run each proposed activity through your core values.

Once you've harnessed your passion, outlined your purpose, and developed your philosophy, you are ready to implement a plan. Start looking at the specifics such as event calendaring and curriculum. Assemble a key group of girls who are willing to serve as your sounding board. Run your ideas by them and empower them to help you accomplish your purpose.

Passion, purpose, philosophies, and plans are meaningless without the pursuit of God and His glory. Sadly, He is often the missing link to successful ministry. Let the greatest aim of your girls' ministry be to know God and bring Him glory.❀

J. Merritt Johnston is the President and Cofounder of SAGE Ministries. She also serves as the Director of Women's Ministries at Lake Pointe Church in Rockwall, Texas.

Reprinted from *Leading Student Ministry, Spring 2005.* Used by Permission.

Counseling Basics

by Tony Rankin

TEEN GIRLS EXPERIENCE emotional highs and lows that strike fear in the hearts of most adults. *Wild About You* may bring up some emotional struggles with the girls in your group. You may be asked to do some version of interacting that will include some of the same skills, issues, and compassion that qualified Christian therapists provide their clients. Here are some basic ideas and thoughts that will help prepare you for the counseling opportunities that may be a part of this study.

What to Do, What Not to Do

- Avoid taking on issues that you are not qualified to handle. This is mentioned first because many youth workers and mentors can get in way over their heads in a counseling situation.
- Refuse to do one-on-one "counseling" in private. Closed doors without windows can lead to situations that are not healthy in a counseling relationship—even among women.
- Don't become the therapist or the doctor.
- Know when to refer to a professional.

Things to Keep in Mind

One of the important factors in counseling teenagers is recognizing the various kinds of relationships that require extra attention. Youth workers need to maintain a proper balance between being safely detached from the student's problems to becoming emotionally attached with the student.

Safety Issues—Teenagers love caring adults and are drawn to the ones who talk, listen, and love. You as the leader must be able to recognize the difference between trust and poor judgment. Both leaders and students want to be trusted and to be trustworthy. A blind trust and failure to see the red flags have horrible consequences.

Be aware of the kinds of touches you give and receive from the students you encounter. Needy students who idolize the compassionate student worker can misinterpret many touches. Second, offering rides to individual girls carries with it a high risk as well (and it doesn't matter which gender is involved). Third, waiting around for the last girl to be picked up is dangerous. Refuse to wait by yourself. Always have another adult present.

Balance—Maintaining a sense of life balance is crucial in helping with the needs and hurts of girls. A volunteer student worker can often feel unappreciated. (Very few students actually stop and thank you for all that you do in ministry with them.) Feeling unappreciated pitted against the desire to make a real impact in girls' lives can cause you to forget that you have a life outside of the girls' ministry. Keep a balance between giving to teens and your own nourishment.

Practical Tips

Helping students requires a comprehensive approach because each situation is different. Here are some things to consider when helping a student in crisis:

a. Listen. God gives you two ears and only one mouth for a reason. Listen to girls' pain, hurt, confusion, words, and nonverbal expressions of loss or agony. When we listen, we are more able to learn about what is really going on.

b. Talk. When a student shares a problem with you or sits (or stands) in front of you, she is probably waiting for a response. Avoid the clichés like, "Just pray about it" or "Hang in there." Instead, respond with "I think I know what you are going through" (if you really do), "That sounds painful," or offer any suggestions that seem appropriate.

c. Ask how they feel. Phrases such as "Tell me how you feel" or "Tell me what makes you feel sad/happy" are easy places to start.

d. Show that you care. In concrete terms do something for them. Ask them to tell you what they need, or say, "To show you how much I care for you, I want to ..."

e. Admit your humanity. Don't worry if you can't fix it all. No minister or therapist can either. Don't make the situation worse by choosing to "know it all." If you don't know something, admit it.

f. Demonstrate respect. One aspect of an encouraging response to the needs of a student is maintaining respect for the person regardless of his or her background, choices, or feelings about receiving help. Do not miss the significance of this tip. We all have certain biases that color our thinking and attitudes. It is important that we address the sin in a situation but not condemn the sinner. Jesus modeled this beautifully in John 8:1-8.

g. Support, but don't rescue. Ministering to a student effectively will necessitate being nurturing instead of being a caretaker. If you're rescuing, you'll try to take over and make decisions for the girl and treat her as a helpless, fragile individual. You are a resource, and encourager, and a support, not the decision-maker for her. She must choose how to act.

h. Be the adult, not a buddy. Lots of adults think that being a mentor to students means being buddies or friends. However, the most effective way to help hurting students is not to try to be someone cool who hangs out with students. Remember, you're the adult in the situation. Act like one. Teens have friends. They need adults who will step into their lives and be leaders.

i. Be accepting. This does not mean that you approve of girls' decisions and choices. Rather, it means to be accepting of the person who God created regardless of the situation. This allows you the chance to love the student whether or not you know what the problem is.

j. Be an active listener. Paying attention to spoken words, non-verbal responses, and facial expressions will result in hearing the whole story. Often students will not use the same words as adults would to tell the struggles in their lives. When talking with girls, take notice of things like tone of voice, body posture, nervous twitches, and eye contact. They tell the untold story.

k. Relate your story. It's OK to tell students about struggles you've had that relate to the issue a teen is facing. However, be careful about telling the gory details about your past. Most often your story distracts them from their pain and may interfere with their need to tell you details.

If you decide to relate part of your life struggles, be sure you have processed your pain appropriately and that you have reconciled your situation fully. Most importantly, be sure it really matters and would make a difference in the other person's life. The trade-off must be well worth the chance of transparency. It is important to be real, but remember, the focus of the counseling is about helping the other individual, not you. You need to work through issues before counseling others.

l. Deal with emotions. The best way to address feelings is to allow the girl to express them and then refuse to rescue her from the painful experience at hand. You will need to find ways to matter-of-factly deal with the emotions of the student. You may be "going crazy" on the inside, but your outward appearance needs to be calm, caring, and compassionate. You do not have to take on her emotions, agree with them, or even understand them, but you must allow her to express her own feelings and thoughts.

l. Confront with compassion and respect. Lovingly meet the issues of students head-on and avoid ridiculing them. Girls are not fragile dolls that break when we discuss the realities of their choices or life circumstances. Jesus was great at confronting a person's pain and bad choices without demeaning them or making them feel horrible.

m. Assess problems and fears. Learn to use the phrase "You feel ____________ because __________________." If you are right with your judgment, teens will be pleasantly surprised with your ability to detect troubles. If you are wrong, girls will generally correct you and more accurately explain how they are really feeling.

n. Lead girls to explore their world. Girls need to be guided to discover what they don't fully realize or understand. You may need to help them identify and express their inner thoughts and emotions—they may not yet be able to put a label on what they're feeling. Once you've identified what's really going on, you'll be able to deal with the situation and address their issues.

• ***Know when to refer.*** Occasionally you will get in over your head and will need to encourage a teen girl to seek additional help from a professional counselor. Situations may include rape, sexual or physical abuse, drug or alcohol abuse, legal difficulties, assaults, emotional issues, and physical problems. Avoid trying to be "Student Minister of the Year" or "Leader of the Month" by maintaining rapport with the girl and failing to communicate your concerns to her family. Your job is to minister to the whole family, not just the student. Keeping a secret from parents may have horrible consequences and negatively impact the family.

You need to be aware of your local and state laws regarding disclosure of abuse. In most states, if you are told firsthand of an abusive situation involving a minor, you are required to report that to the authorities.

In instances of illegal behavior, you will also need to let girls know beforehand that if they disclose illegal behavior they are involved in, you will be under obligation to report that to their parents or another trusted authority. You need to have ground rules for disclosure that those whom you counsel understand fully. Never, ever agree that you "won't tell a soul." You'll end up in a double-bind, caught between your promise and the legal guidelines of reporting to authorities.

You may be the first or last person to whom students tell their secrets. Accept the opportunity to counsel with students as a privilege and honor. Listen, give your time, pray about your guidance, and refer whenever necessary. Love and respect students enough to help them the best way possible, even when you are not the right person to assist them. Ministering to students and their families during a time of crisis may make a life-changing difference. Take the chance.❀

Tony Rankin is a clinical therapist in Nashville, Tennessee, and the Family Ministry Specialist for the Tennessee Baptist Convention.

Adapted from "Counseling Ministry 101," which appeared in *Leading Student Ministry, Spring 2005*. Used with permission.

SESSION 1

Am I Invisible or What?

Supplies and Resources
- [ ] *Wild About You* student book
- [ ] *Wild About You* DVD, cued to Segment 1
- [ ] Pens
- [ ] Bibles
- [ ] TV/DVD player
- [ ] Superhero cartoon clips (optional)
- [ ] Your high school yearbook (optional)
- [ ] Note cards
- [ ] Paper (optional)
- [ ] *The Princess Diaries* movie (optional)

Introduction: Superheroes
As girls arrive, greet them and introduce yourself to any visitors. If girls do not know each other, provide time for girls to tell their names, where they go to school, and if they have any siblings. Then ask: **When you were a child, what cartoons did you watch? Did you ever watch cartoons about superheroes such as Superman, Batman, or Spiderman? Who was your favorite superhero? Why? If you could have any superpower what would it be?** *(super strength, flying, reading people's minds, seeing through objects, spinning a web, becoming invisible)* **What would you want to do with that superpower?**

After girls have had a chance to talk about their childhood dreams, ask: **What would be the advantage of being invisible? Where would you want to go or what would you want to do if you could remain invisible?** Then ask: **Can being invisible be a bad thing? Why or why not? Can you be invisible in the middle of a crowd? Why or why not? Can you be lonely in the middle of a crowd? Explain.** Say: **Sometimes teen girls feel invisible. They feel like no one really notices who they are or cares about them. We'll be talking about that today.**

Cartoon Clip (option)
As girls arrive, play cartoon clips of superheroes. Many discount stores carry inexpensive cartoons, or you may know of someone who has one. If you choose to play a video, make sure your church has secured a license for viewing such clips. [Most videos begin with a notice stating the video is intended for Home Use Only. Some face-to-face teaching activities are fair use, but your church may want or need to obtain a license to show videos and films publicly. A license may be obtained through Christian Video Licensing International (CVLI) at 1-888-771-2854 or *www.cvli.org.*] After all the girls have arrived and have watched some of the cartoons, continue with the discussion questions in "Introduction: Superheroes."

When I Feel Invisible
Say: **Let's take a quick quiz to evaluate how invisible you may feel.** Direct girls to take the "What's Your IQ—Invisibility Quotient?" quiz on page 7 of the student book. After several minutes, review their responses. Ask: **What situations make you feel the most invisible?** After girls respond, say: **Let's explore what situations might make us feel invisible.** Direct

girls to stand up and form a group in the middle of the room. Designate one side of the room as "very much" and the other side as "not at all." Explain that these sides form two ends of a continuum with an imaginary line between them. You'll read a series of scenarios, and girls will stand along the continuum to indicate how much each of the scenarios makes them feel invisible. Read the following situations or create your own based on your knowledge of the group:

1. A cute guy asks you if you think your best friend would go out with him.
2. You and your sister both come home with good grades. Your mom and dad seem excited at your sister's grades, but they don't seem to care about yours.
3. You drop your books in the hallway at school and nobody stops to help you pick them up.
4. When your dad comes home from work, he plops down in his recliner and barely talks to you the rest of the evening.
5. You're hanging out with a group of friends when some guys start talking about how cute the new girl is.
6. You've been down in the dumps for several weeks but nobody has asked what's wrong.

Direct girls to sit down. Ask: **How many of you have experienced similar situations?** Allow girls to share their experiences. Then say: **Lots of girls feel invisible.** Read the question and quotes from "Instant Message" on page 16 in the student book. Allow girls to discuss the quotes. Allow girls to share any other similar stories. To initiate discussion, you might want to share a story from your teen years that highlights how you felt invisible. You might even want to bring your yearbook to the session for girls to see how you might have felt invisible because of your physical appearance.

Video Viewing

Introduce the video by explaining the following: **This study is based on a book called** *Do You Think I'm Beautiful?* **and it was written by a woman named Angela Thomas. As you'll see in this video, she's felt very much like you have—like nobody really notices you.** Play Segment 1 of the DVD. Allow for discussion. Ask questions such as: **Which of your school pictures do you hate the most? Why? Which is your favorite? Why? Angela says in the video that in junior high, nobody wants to be different. Everyone wants to be like everyone else. Do you agree? Why or why not? Does that change when you get to high school? Why or why not? Which one of the BarlowGirls do you relate to the best? Why? Is it encouraging to you that someone like her has wrestled with the same struggles you have? Why or why not? Which of the characters in the Cinderella story do you identify with the most? Why? Which of the characters would you allow yourself to become? Why?**

Not Invisible

Print each of the following Scripture references on separate note cards: Job 19:14; Psalm 13:1; Psalm 25:16; Psalm 31:12a; Psalm 42:9a; and Isaiah 49:15. Say: **Even people in the Bible felt invisible.** Distribute the note cards among the girls in your group and instruct them to read the Scriptures aloud. Ask: **Which Scripture do you relate to the least? Why? Which Scripture do you identify with the most? Why?**

Say: **There was a woman in the New Testament who probably felt invisible.** Direct girls to turn to Luke 8:42-48 in their Bibles. Call on one girl to read it. Summarize for girls the information in the student book under "Living as an Invisible" on page 10 of the student book. Then group girls into pairs and direct them to write a journal entry as the woman the day before she met

Jesus. They can record their work in the student books. After several minutes, call on girls to share their journal entries.

Say: **This woman must have been petrified around that crowd of people. However, when you're feeling alone and forgotten, you'll do what it takes. Notice what happened after she touched Jesus' robe. He noticed. He asked who touched Him. And it scared the woman.** Call on a girl to read Luke 8:47. Say: **Did you catch that? She was trying to slip into and out of the crowd unnoticed. She was trying to remain invisible. She was used to it. After all this time, nobody paid attention to her. But she was encountering no ordinary person; she was encountering God. And to God, nobody is anonymous. Nobody is invisible. And that includes you!**

Noticed and Loved

Ask: **What are some ways God has shown us that we're not invisible to Him?** (*He made us each uniquely; He answers our prayers; He gives peace; He provides friends; He protects and cares for us*) Direct girls to read the poem "I Am" on page 8 of the student book. Ask: **Have you ever felt like this? What could you say to her to encourage her?**

As an option, group girls into teams of three or four. Provide paper and pens. Direct teams to write their own poem of encouragement in response to the "I Am" poem. Explain that the poems do not have to rhyme or even keep the same cadence. Also give them the option of turning their poems into songs. After several minutes, allow teams to share their poems. Ask: **Does knowing that we're not invisible give you any greater peace about who you are? Why or why not?**

Say: **Next week, we'll learn that not only does God see us, but He loves us more deeply than we can even comprehend.** Before ending the Bible study, point out the other features in the student book, such as the "Ask Angela" column and the "In My Own Words" section. To close in prayer, direct girls to offer a sentence prayer, thanking God that they're not invisible.

Before girls leave, make sure you have secured information about all of them, including home phone numbers, cell phone numbers, and e-mail addresses. Also explain that their friends can still join in the study. Encourage them to bring a friend next week. Remember, all women wrestle with these issues!

Over the next week, call or e-mail the girls and thank them for being a part of the study. If you know of other girls who would benefit from the study or would like to join in, remind them to come next week. Also during the next week, preview video segment 2.

Princess Lessons (option)

To end your time together, watch the movie *The Princess Diaries* (Rated G, Walt Disney Pictures) together. Discuss with girls how they have felt like Mia. You might even want to kick off the study with a slumber party, showing this movie as a highlight of the evening.❀

session 2

What Does God See in Me Anyway?

Supplies and Resources
- ☐ *Wild About You* student book
- ☐ *Wild About You* DVD, cued to Segment 2
- ☐ Pens
- ☐ Bibles
- ☐ TV/DVD player
- ☐ White pieces of paper
- ☐ Construction paper
- ☐ Art supplies
- ☐ Markers

Introduction

As the girls arrive, play a video clip from a TV show or movie in which a male character calls his girlfriend or wife by an endearing nickname such as "sweetheart" or "dear." The nickname can even be funny. After the group has watched the clip, ask girls if they noticed the nickname the man used for his beloved. Ask: **Have you ever heard your dad call your mom by a name like that? Why do couples use nicknames like that for each other? What is a nickname you have now? What was a nickname you had growing up? How did you get that name? Where do nicknames come from? What do they tell us about people?** Say: **Most of the time, nicknames are terms of affection. They communicate love, affection, and even deep commitment.** Use an example from your own experience with your husband or a close family member to demonstrate how terms such as "darling" or "sweet pea" communicate deep love. Ask: **If God were to use a nickname with you, what word do you think He would choose?** Allow girls to wrestle with this question. It will challenge their thinking about how God views them. Then ask: **Was it difficult to think of a nickname that God would choose for you? Why or why not? Is it a stretch for you to think that God would love you on such a personal level? Why or why not?**

Say: **Before we move on to learning how God really feels about us, it might be helpful for us to examine how we think God feels about us.** Direct girls to complete the quiz on page 26 of the student book. Afterward, ask: **What did you learn about yourself? Do you think you are accurate in what God thinks about you? Why or why not?** Say: **Sometimes our own preconceived ideas about God prevent us from seeing ourselves through His eyes.**

God's Nickname for Us

Call on a girl to read the first three paragraphs of the "Deeper" section on page 28. Once it's read, say: **One section bears repeating. It is: "Here's some great news: The God who slung the stars across the heavens… whose very breath gives life … that God, the King has always been taken with you. He thinks you're gorgeous. In fact, He is absolutely wild about you!"** Say: **Today, we'll be learning more about how God really views us. It may be a staggering truth to learn, but it can change the course of your life.**

Video Viewing

Play Segment 2 of the DVD. Afterward, discuss the video by asking: **In the video, Angela said, "The King, God Almighty, Maker of heaven and earth, the One who flung the stars across the sky, He is the one who dreamed you up." Does that change your perception of yourself? Why or why not? Have you ever had an experience when someone noticed you and you weren't a wallflower anymore? How did that feel? How does it feel knowing that God created you exactly as He designed—crooked nose, freckles, short, tall, brown hair, blue eyes—all perfectly in His plan? Was it difficult to believe what Angela said? Why or why not? Could you identify with Alyssa of BarlowGirl when she talked about feeling plain and invisible? If so, how?** Then say: **Let's look at some Scripture to find out if what Angela said is really true.**

Enthralled with You

Call on a girl to read Psalm 45:10-11 from the *New International Version* of the Bible. Say: **This verse is highlighted in your magazine on page 28.** Ask: **What does it say about the king? What does it mean to be enthralled?** Say: **To help us understand how cool that word is, let's find some synonyms for it. Direct girls to do the exercise on page 28 to discover some words that mirror enthralled.** After a couple of minutes, highlight the words, allowing girls to discuss which one is the most meaning to them. Then ask: **Does it seem strange to think that God is enthralled with you? Why or why not? Does it seem strange to think that anyone would think of you that way? Why or why not?** Say: **In fact, Psalm 45:11 can be translated as "The King is wild for you!"** (*THE MESSAGE*) Ask: **What does it mean to be wild about someone? Does it blow your mind to think that God cares that deeply for you? Why or why not?** Say: **The fact is that Scripture tells us over and**

over that God is that passionate and crazy about you and me.

Digging In

If you have enough girls, direct them to get into pairs or groups of three. Give each of the groups one of the following Scripture references: Isaiah 49:14-16; Psalm 139:13-16; Isaiah 43:1-4; Ephesians 3:17-19; Isaiah 63:9. If you have a small number of girls, give each girl one of the Scriptures. Also distribute pieces of paper and markers. Direct them to read their passages and to create a poster that illustrates what each Scripture says about how God feels about them. After several minutes, call on girls or teams to read each passage and to share their posters.

Ask: **What did Isaiah mean we he wrote that God had engraved Israel on the palms of His hands (Isa. 49:16)? What does this tell you about God's character? Do you think God would ever forget you? Even in the small things? Why or why not?** Say: **In Isaiah 43:1-4, what was the underlying theme?** (*God would be with the nation of Israel and would not let it be destroyed because He loved them.*) Recent surveys indicate that teens know God exists, but they think He is not involved in their everyday lives. Help girls recognize that God is very involved in their lives, not just a passive bystander. Explain that in fact, He has been active in their lives from before they were even born. Highlight Psalm 139:14-16. Ask: **How does this psalm encourage you?** Say: **God's love was demonstrated in your very conception and birth. In fact, His love for you is too great to measure.** Call on a girl to read Ephesians 3:17-19. Ask: **What does this passage tell you about God's love?**

Not Just a Number

Keep girls in their groups (if you have a large number of girls) and give the following assignment: **You've received a note from a friend which reads:** *I heard your youth minister say at church that God loves me. But He loves me just like He's loved every other created person in the history of the universe. I'm just one among zillions.* Direct girls to read "Inside and Out" in their books on page 31 and to create a note in response, telling the friend why God doesn't love her just like zillions of others. After several minutes, allow girls or groups of girls to share their letters. Ask: **How do you feel knowing that God loves you with this kind of intensity? Has there ever been a time in your life when you were acutely aware of God's love? How has God shown you that He loves you personally? How can you and I recognize times when God is trying to show His love in a personal way? What might His love look like?**

Closing

Provide art supplies. Say: **Today, I want you to create something as a reminder of how God views you.** Call on a girl to read Luke 1:28. Then explain that *The Message* translates this verse as: "Good Morning! You're beautiful with God's beauty, beautiful inside and out!" Explain that God feels the same way about them as He did about Mary, the mother of Jesus. Explain that you have provided some craft materials for them to create signs to remind them of God's opinion of them. Direct them to use either Luke 1:28 or Psalm 45:10-11 as a model.

For example, if a girl chose Luke 1:28, her sign would read as follows: "Good morning, _____ (fill in their name)! You're beautiful with God's beauty, beautiful inside and out!" Psalm 45:10-11 would read: "The King is enthralled by _____'s (fill in the name) beauty!" Girls may want to choose another Scripture studied today. Help them to individualize their choice of Scripture.

Encourage girls to take time to decorate the signs and personalize them by adding finishing touches that speak to their own individuality and personality. You might want to create a sign of your own as an example. Allow the girls to show off their signs, explaining why they choose that particular verse and why they choose do decorate it as they did. Encourage girls to place these signs on the mirror in their bathrooms or in their lockers at school as a reminder that God is wild about them.

Direct each girl to choose one of the passages that was particularly special to them. For the closing prayer, each girl will pray the Scripture back to God in thanksgiving for how He views them. If a girl chose Isaiah 49:14-16, she might pray, "Lord, thank you that you have not forsaken me and that you have not forgotten me. Thank you that you love me like a mother loves a child. Thank you for caring so much about me that you've engraved me on the palm of your hand." A girl who chooses Psalm 139:14-16 might pray, "Thank you for putting me together in my mother's womb, for wonderfully making me, for caring enough to know everything about me, even as I was woven together in the secret place." If time allows, give the girls opportunity to write out their prayers so they have an opportunity to think through them. If time does not permit, direct girls to pray the Scripture from their Bibles. Then close the prayer time by thanking God for being wild about you and the girls.�֍

Session 3

The Voices of Other Loves

Supplies and Resources
- ☐ *Wild About You* student book
- ☐ *Wild About You* DVD, cued to Segment 3
- ☐ Pens
- ☐ Bibles
- ☐ TV/DVD player
- ☐ Handheld or hand-size mirrors for each girl (available at a dollar store)
- ☐ Paper
- ☐ Pencils

Introduction

As girls arrive, show a movie clip of a girl who gets distracted when a guy enters the room. Make sure the movie is appropriate for this setting. After the clip, say: **Sometimes it's easy to become distracted by guys. They can get the best of us. The problem is that guys can be such a distraction that they pull us away from God. Because we're so focused on "him" we lose sight of a greater love than his—the love of God. Today, we'll be talking about the things that distract us from God's love.**

Video

Play Segment 3 from the DVD. Afterward, ask: **What three distractions did Angela talk about?** *(fathers, boys, and girlfriends)* **Do you think these are common distractions for girls? Why or why not? What other things can be real distractions for girls?** *(popularity, clothes, sports, money, etc.)* **What point** was Angela trying to make using the water illustration? What did you learn from her story about the dinner reception at the wedding? What were some of the ways the Barlow sisters deal with those distractions? Do you think you could do that in your own life? Why or why not?** Then say: **Let's talk a little more about the things that pull you away from God's love.**

Quiz

Say: **You may be pulled away so easily by other loves that you don't even realize it's happening. A quiz might help you determine what distracts you the easiest.** Direct girls to complete the quiz on page 47. Allow girls to share which thing pulls them away from God the easiest. Ask: **Is there another distraction that causes more problems than these three? If so, what is it?** Say: **Today, we'll be focusing on three major things that can keep us from recognizing and living in God's untamable love for us—guys, our dads, and our friends.**

The Root Problem

Ask: **Is it a problem to want to date a guy, to have a good relationship with your dad, or to have great friendships?** *(no)* Say: **The problem is that we misplace the priority of these things and they become bigger than life. We think that these things are all we need. But we're created for more than that.**

Distribute the hand mirrors. (If you cannot secure enough mirrors, take the girls to a nearby mirror or ask girls to bring one to the study this week.) Direct girls to find the Scripture on page 49 of the student book. Instruct one of the girls to read it out loud by placing it in front of mirror so she can see it clearly. Ask: **What does this verse tell us about ourselves?** *(God created us in His image and His likeness)* Ask: **Why was the mirror helpful? What's the purpose of a mirror?** Say: **A mirror reflects what is in front of it. According to this passage, you and I are made in God's image. In other words, we reflect our Creator. We mirror a little bit of who He is. One way we are made in His image is in our capacity and need for relationship. We're created for relationships—primarily and most importantly, a relationship with God, the One who made us.** Ask: **How does it make you feel to know that you were created for the express purpose of knowing and magnifying God?** *(excited, nervous, apathetic, unsure, insecure, overjoyed, unworthy, overwhelmed)*

Say: **Nothing else in all of creation has the capacity for communion with God like you and me. And that's why a relationship with God is so important in our lives. The problem is that other things get in the way of that relationship. These things should point us back to our Heavenly Father, but sometimes these things get in the way of Him.**

Boys, Boys, Boys

Ask: **Have you ever been around a girl who has fallen head over heels for a guy? How did she act? Did her behavior bother you? Why or why not? What are some silly ways you've acted around guys? Why did you react that way?** Say: **It's easy for girls to think that a guy could make them happy or complete.** Call on a girl to read John 4:1-18. Ask: **What do we learn about this woman? What do her past relationships reveal about her? What did Jesus' reaction to her tell you about His character?** Say: **This woman was searching**

for something that could fill her soul. Instead of seeking after God, she sought the love of a man to make her whole. Obviously, she was still searching. Discuss with girls the ending of this story, pointing out the Samaritan woman's proclamation that she had found the Messiah. Say: **Many girls will go from relationship to relationship, offering their hearts and bodies to guys in exchange for love. The only problem is that human love can never replace the love of God. Human love is incomplete. No matter how hard we may try, that love will never satisfy our souls because our souls were created for more.**

Direct girls to their student books to the section "In the Right Place" on page 51 and instruct them to fill in the blanks with the correct words to discover the need for prioritizing relationships with guys. After several minutes, ask: **How can a growing love relationship with God actually help you in your relationships with guys?** *(He can lead them to date the right guys, or to evaluate when a guy is not good for them)* Ask: **Why do you think girls go so overboard when it comes to the opposite gender? Who is someone who's been a role model for you in keeping guys in proper perspective? What did you learn from her?**

As an option, invite an older college student to come speak to the girls about her successes and/or failures in keeping opposite gender relationships in their proper place. Invite her to share lessons she has learned about what happens when a guy gets in the way of God.

The Other Man

Say: **Some of you have a great relationship with your dad, and that allows you to see a little bit of God's love. Our fathers are supposed to mirror for us the love of God. However, some of you may come from tough backgrounds, from broken or even abusive** families, and it's tough to understand God's love if He's supposed to be like a father. Call on a girl to read the first portion of "Love on the Line" on page 59 of their books in which a girl writes a letter to God. Ask: **What would you tell this girl if she let you read this letter? What feelings do you hear in her letter? How have you felt like this girl? How are you different from her?**

Call on a two girls to read Psalm 27:10 and Psalm 68:5. Discuss how these verses can help girls who are struggling with understanding God as their Father. Give girls a piece of paper and a pencil. Direct girls to respond to the letter they read earlier in the student book. After several minutes, allow girls to share their letters, and call on one girl to read God's letter in response. Ask: **What stuck out to you in God's letter of response? How does this letter show a part of God's character?**

Girls, Girls, Girls

Call on girls to name some qualities of a good friend. Lead girls to give examples of those qualities in their friendships. Then direct them to name some things that will tear apart a friendship, such as jealousy, anger, unrealistic expectations, and so forth. Allow them to share times when those things hurt a friendship they had. Say: **One major thing that will wound a friendship is your high expectations. Sure, you desire certain things from friends, such as trust, loyalty, and confidentiality. But if you're expecting a friend to meet your every need and to make your life perfect, then you're headed for real trouble.** If appropriate, share a time in your life when these expectations caused a conflict in one of your friendships. Help girls to recognize that a friend's love is designed to point us to God's love, not be a replacement for it.

Confession Time

Say: **In the video, Angela pointed out that guys, our dads, and our friends should give us a healthy taste of the love of God, but that they were never intended to fill us up. Why do you think so many people look to these things to fill them instead of God?**

Challenge girls to think about the things they pursue that tear them away from God's love. Allow for some quiet time of reflection. Challenge girls to confess to God those areas in which they struggle. Allow girls to share with one another if they feel comfortable. Then close in prayer, asking God to make His love real and personal to them this week. As girls leave, point out the feature articles and other elements in the student magazine that will help them further explore the distractions they face in experiencing God's amazing love for them.

After the Bible study, you may want to hang around to talk with girls who may be struggling with accepting God's untamable love for them. As this Bible study begins to unfold, girls may confront their own insecurity and fears. Be watchful for girls who may be experiencing anxiety or discomfort at discussing these topics. You may want to spend some time with these girls on an individual basis over the next few weeks. Don't be alarmed, either, if God begins to deal in your own heart about the misconceptions you have held about Him. Be honest with girls as God teaches and heals you.❁

Session 4

Whispers of Unbelief

Supplies and Resources
- [ ] *Wild About You* student book
- [ ] *Wild About You* DVD, cued to Segment 4
- [ ] Pens
- [ ] Bibles
- [ ] TV/DVD player
- [ ] Magazines and newspapers
- [ ] Prize for winner of quiz
- [ ] Video of extreme sports or stunts (optional)
- [ ] Two pieces of paper
- [ ] Tape
- [ ] Poster with common fears listed (optional)
- [ ] Large rock smoothed by erosion
- [ ] Music to play during closing

Introduction

As girls arrive, distribute magazines and newspapers. Instruct girls to look through the media to find stories of people doing dangerous or scary activities, such as climbing a mountain, skydiving, flying in a hot air balloon, and so forth. Allow teens to determine their own definition of fear.

After most girls have arrived, call on girls to highlight the examples they found. Allow girls to comment on whether or not they would do each activity. Then ask: **What's the scariest thing you've ever done? What's the scariest, most extreme activity you've ever heard about? When you were a child, what were you afraid of? What are you afraid of now?** *(the dark, spiders, looking stupid, etc.)* Say: **Fears can come from lots of sources.** Direct girls to turn to the quiz on page 67 to see how much they know about phobias. Award a prize to the girl with the most correct answers. Then explain: **Today, we'll discover how fear can keep us from experiencing God's love.**

Video (option)

As an option, play a video of extreme sports, stunts, or activities as the girls look through the magazines. You might even want to show scenes from TV shows that challenge people's fears. Allow them to comment on the video and which situations would be the most scary to them.

Scary Scale (option)

This activity can replace the opening activity that uses newspapers and magazines. Prior to the lesson, print the number 1 on one piece of paper, and the number 10 on another. Tape these numbers on opposite walls in your meeting room. As girls arrive, call attention to the numbers and explain that you will read a series of activities. They are to indicate how scary that activity is to them by moving anywhere between the 1 and the 10.

For example, if the activity is not very scary, a girl may stand near the number 1. If it's a little scary, a girl can stand in the middle of the room between the two numbers, indicating ambivalence. Standing by the number 10 indicates that the activity is very scary to the girl. Read the following scenarios. After each is named, discuss with girls why it got the rating they chose. Then move on to the next scenario.

- Giving a speech at school explaining why you're a Christian
- Hiking to the top of Mount Everest
- Going to college in another state
- Moving to a foreign country to be a missionary
- Snowboarding down a black diamond
- Racing a car on a NASCAR® track
- Telling your mom the truth about the money you stole
- Staying by yourself in the house over the weekend
- Witnessing to your teammates
- Telling your boyfriend that you want to remain sexually pure

After reading all the scenarios, say: **This exercise was intended for you to look at some fears you may have. Fear can be a powerful thing. It even can keep us from realizing that God is wild about us. Instead of living in God's love, we can live in fear. Today, we'll be discussing the way to deal with fear.**

Quiz Time

Say: **To help you think about fear, complete the quiz on page 66 of your student magazine.** After several minutes, allow girls to share which fear grips them the most. You might need to make them feel more comfortable by first sharing with them the fear that entraps you.

Where Fear Comes From

Say: **The truth about fear is this: left unchecked, it can take over your life. It can whisper into your soul like a quiet disease and can leave you spiritually crippled and paralyzed. Fear can rob you of the truth about yourself and lead you to think that you can't**

possibly be beautiful, especially to God. Fear sounds like this: "There's no way God can really love me. I've messed up too much." or "I'll never be good enough." Do you ever ask yourself, "What if they don't like me?" or "What if I look stupid?" Those statements are steeped in fear—fear of not fitting in, measuring up, or being loved; fear of looking stupid and messing up; and fear of being unworthy of God's affection.**

Display the rock. Allow girls to pass it around the circle and notice its smooth texture. Ask: **Where do these fears about yourself come from?** Say: **Most of the time, they are formed over time, a little bit here and there—like the way water eroded the rock that you held. Fears come into your life bit by bit, eroding your trust in God. These fears are shaped by different factors.**

To help girls recognize where fears come from, instruct them to complete the activity on page 69 of their student magazine. After several minutes, allow girls to share what they wrote if they feel comfortable. You might even want to share some experiences from your own life as appropriate. Then say: **Recognizing the source of fears is an important first step. Dealing with those fears is another important step.**

How to Deal with Fear

Ask: **Have you ever been afraid of something, only to discover what you were afraid of wasn't really a big deal?** Allow girls to share their experiences, such as taking a test, facing discipline from parents, and so forth. Then say: **When you face your fear, some of its power is taken away. When you ignore fear, it can become a stronghold in your life. A stronghold is simply something that has a strong hold on you. So let's face the fears.** Form four teams if your group size will allow for it. If not, distribute the following assignments to individuals or pairs.

Team 1. You've heard a friend say she's afraid God can't really love her because of her mistakes. Using Romans 8:38-39, give her some advice about God's love.

Team 2. You've heard a friend talk about how she fears blending into the crowd because she's not really unique or special. Using Psalm 139:13-16, give her some advice about what God sees in her.

Team 3. You've heard a friend talk about how she doesn't want to follow God because she's afraid of being rejected by people. Using Galatians 1:10, give her some advice about following God.

Team 4. You've heard a friend talk about how she doesn't think she can measure up. Using Colossians 1:21-22, give her some advice about how God sees her.

After several minutes, call on girls or teams of girls to read their scenario, the Scripture passage, and their response. After each team shares, discuss the verses to make sure girls understand how those verses deal with the fear and help them to experience more fully God's love for them.

DVD Segment

Play Segment 4 of the DVD. After the video, lead in a discussion by asking: **How are you like the prodigal in Angela's story? How are you not like him? Why is it so hard for us to return to God sometimes? What do we sometimes tell ourselves about God when we're in the distant country?** *(God can't forgive me; God will be disappointed in me, so I can't return; God will punish me too much, etc.)* **What did Angela say might happen if we stay away from God too long?** *(we become a slave to fear)* **Where does that fear really come from?** *(Satan)* **Do you agree with Angela that**

Satan targets young women like you early? Why or why not? What illustrations did Angela use to talk about God's limitless mercy? *(fish in a stream, air rationing)* **How do you feel knowing that you can never use up God's love? According to Angela, what takes the place of fear?** *(God's love)* **Why can love and fear not be compatible?**

Then summarize by saying: **Every girl fears fading in to the background, looking stupid, and failing to measure up. To believe that she is valued, loved, beautiful is just too unbelievable. Maybe no one in this world has ever called you beautiful. Maybe you've made lots of mistakes. Maybe you have been embarrassed, shamed, or ridiculed—and that has left you feeling unloved, unwanted, unworthy. But here's the really big deal: You look into the mirror with YOUR eyes. That's the problem. But God doesn't see as you see (or as the world sees). He never has. He sees through perfect eyes and He sees you as beautiful all the way around.**

Facing Your Fear

Say: **The only way to deal with fears is to face them.** Direct girls to spread apart in the room to find some privacy. Play some quiet music for reflection. Challenge them to think about the fears that keep them from truly experiencing God's love. After a few minutes of reflection, direct girls to complete the activity on page 70 by writing a note to God about their fears. After more time of quiet reflection and journaling, call girls back together. If the girls are willing, close the prayer time by allowing the girls to voice their written prayers to God. If they don't feel comfortable with this, close in a group prayer, asking God to help you and the girls to face your fears instead of allowing fear to dominate your life.❀

SESSION 5

What Lies Do I Believe?

Supplies and Resources
- [ ] *Wild About You* student book
- [ ] *Wild About You* DVD, cued to Segment 5
- [ ] Pens
- [ ] Bibles
- [ ] TV/DVD player
- [ ] Magazines
- [ ] TV listings
- [ ] Movie listings
- [ ] Paper
- [ ] Markers
- [ ] Team assignments

Introduction
As the girls arrive, explain that they will take a quick test. Read the following statements and direct teens to determine whether the statements are true or false. (Taken from *www.snopes.com.*)

1. A woman tries to smuggle into the U.S. by hiding in a car's dashboard. (true)
2. If you throw a frog in boiling water he will quickly jump out. But if you put a frog in a pan of cold water and raise the temperature ever so slowly, the frog will adjust to the temperature because it is cold-blooded, and it will literally boil to death. (false)
3. Water in a toilet rotates counterclockwise in the northern hemisphere and clockwise in the southern hemisphere. This is due to the Coriolis Effect, caused by the rotation of the Earth. (false)
4. Ernest Vincent Wright wrote a novel, *Gadsby,* which contains over 50,000 words—none of them with the letter *E*. (true)
5. A penny left in a glass of Coca-Cola® will dissolve overnight. (false)

Discuss with the girls why they thought each of the false items sounded good to them. Say: **These stories sound true and people believe them without investigating the truth.** Challenge girls to research the Web site cited as a reference to find out the truth about each of the stories. Continue by saying: **In our search to be called beautiful, many of us have bought into lies believing they were truth. Today, we'll discover those lies, the source of those lies, and ways to combat those lies.**

To Tell the Truth (option)
Prior to the lesson, enlist the help of three adults in your church. One of the adults should have a true and interesting fact about himself (learned to fly at age 12, once met the president of the United States, can juggle fire, etc.). The other two volunteers should know about this interesting fact and be able to answer questions as if that fact were true about themselves. As girls arrive, introduce the three guests. Explain that the object of the game is for the girls to discover who the interesting fact is about. (Make sure none of the girls knows this fact.) Allow each of

the girls to ask alternating questions to the three panelists and to listen carefully to the answers. Distribute pieces of paper and markers. Direct girls to write in large letters who they think the fact concerns. Then call on girls to reveal their answers simultaneously. Then, tell who the fact is actually about. Give that volunteer the opportunity to share about his or her skill or interesting fact. Thank your volunteers for their help.

After the game, debrief by asking the following: **Who was most believable? Could you detect the liars? Why or why not? What was hard about discovering the truth?** Then say: **Sometimes it's difficult to tell the truth from a lie.** Say: **In our search to be called beautiful, lots of us have bought into lies believing they were truth. Today, we'll discover those lies, the source of those lies, and ways to combat those lies.**

Magazine Search

Prior to the study, gather magazines, recent editions of TV listings (such as TV Guide or a newspaper listing) and a listing of movies. Say: **One of the major sources of the lies we believe is the media.** Group girls into teams and them the following assignments.

Team 1. Look through the magazines provided to find messages about beauty. Tear out those ads, columns, and articles, and be prepared to share what message each is trying to communicate.

Team 2. Look through the movie listings provided. As a team, discuss the messages about beauty found in some of the movies popular to teen girls. Be prepared to share with the large group the messages those movies are trying to communicate.

Team 3. Look through the TV listings to find shows popular to teen girls. Discuss the

messages about beauty that these TV shows try to communicate. Be prepared to share your work.

As teens are working, circulate among the groups to make sure they understand the assignment. You may also need to provide some examples to get them started. After several minutes, call on each group to share its findings. Then ask: **How much do you think you've bought into these messages? How truthful do you think these messages really are?** Direct girls to look at the cover of the student magazine. Ask: **Does it seem contradictory to talk about the lies culture tells us, but then use a magazine format for this Bible study book? Why or why not? Does the image on the cover bother you? Why or why not?** Say: **Sometimes it's hard to know what's truth and what's a lie, who to trust and who to run from. To begin our search today, let's see how much you've bought into the lies.**

Quiz

Direct girls to take the quiz found on page 86. After several minutes, discuss with girls how well they fared. Then say: **While media play a huge role in our understanding of beauty, the source of these lies runs deeper. Let's discover where these lies originate.**

Digging Deeper

Call on a girl to read John 8:42-44. Ask: **Who's speaking here? What does Jesus say is the source of lying? What do we learn about Satan in this passage?** Then say: **In this story, Jesus was talking to the Pharisees, who had rejected Him as the Messiah. He explained the nature of lies—they come from Satan. Think about it. He lied to Adam and Eve in the beginning and he's been lying ever since. He is your enemy who wants to destroy your life.** Call on two other girls to read John 10:10

and 1 Peter 5:8. Ask: **What else do you learn about the devil?** Then explain: **Satan uses the culture around you to dominate your thinking, to make you believe that you have to look a certain way in order to be valued.**

DVD Segment

Play Segment 5 from the DVD. Afterward, ask: **What did Angela mean when she said Madison Avenue doesn't speak for God? What was Angela's gift that she would love to be able to teach young women?** *(to know the difference between the voice of God and the voice of the Accuser, Satan)* **Why do you think it's so hard for teens to distinguish between the two? Which woman did you relate to the most: the older woman who couldn't hear God's love, or the super model who thought God saw her as ugly on the inside? What did you think when you learned that even a super model struggled? What does that tell you about every person's struggle? We know that we need to listen to God instead of our culture, but how do we do that?**

Listening to the Father

Say: **Lies will dominate your life until you learn to listen to the Truth instead. The lies your culture, the world, and Satan have been telling you will only be stilled by listening to His voice, believing what He says about you.** Call on a girl to read John 10:1-5,27-28. Ask: **What was Jesus trying to communicate in these verses?** *(God's people will listen to and follow God's voice)* **How can you listen to and follow God's voice?** Say: **Listening to and believing what God says about you and your beauty is crucial. But sometimes we have difficulty slowing down enough to listen. Let's take some time today to listen to God's truth.** Direct girls to find a quiet spot alone in the room, away from the others. Call attention to the lies on page 91 of the student magazine. Challenge them to take a few minutes to quiet their

hearts before God, and ask Him to tell them a truth to combat the lies. Call girls back together and allow them to share what truths God revealed to them. Explain that there are no right or wrong answers. When girls have finished sharing, say: **You've learned some important steps in learning to hear God's voice.** Ask: **What did you do?** Allow girls to think through the process they just experienced. Then explain the following steps in discerning truth from a lie.

1. Stop and listen to yourself. What are you telling yourself?
2. Evaluate whether the statement is a truth or a lie based on God's Word.
3. Ask God to show you a truth to combat the lie.
4. Choose to believe God's truth over Satan's lie.

Ask: **What other steps can we take to avoid Satan's trap?** *(spend time with God on a consistent basis; hang out with people who will affirm you; avoid magazines, movies, and TV shows that are a negative influence on you)* Say: **The more time you spend immersed in today's culture, the more you'll begin to be influenced by it. Like a chameleon adapts its skin color to its surroundings, you may begin to adapt your beliefs and actions to the culture around you. That's why it's so important to evaluate the people you spend time with, the music you listen to, the movies and TV shows you watch, and the magazines you read.**

Say: **The One who calls your name is taken with you. The One who knew you before creation is in love with you. To begin to deal with the lies inside your head is to say, "Hey, I won't listen to this anymore. Get that junk out of my way! I want to hear the truth—the music of love, the love song of my Savior." The Beholder is passionate about you.** Close in prayer. ❋

Session 6

Celebrating As the Beloved

Supplies and Resources
- ☐ *Wild About You* student book
- ☐ *Wild About You* DVD, cued to Segment 6
- ☐ Pens
- ☐ Paper
- ☐ Large pieces of paper
- ☐ Tape
- ☐ Markers
- ☐ TV/DVD player
- ☐ Music to play during closing

DVD Opener
As girls arrive, greet them and catch up on what's going on in their lives. Explain that today's study will be a little different and that you all will be watching the DVD segment at the beginning. Play DVD Segment 6. Afterward, discuss the video by asking: **What was in the background when Angela began talking? What does it symbolize for our country? Why would that be important in our discussion of God's amazing love for us?** *(when we begin to believe in and respond from God's love, we find freedom from others' expectations, especially culturally)* **What was the point of her story about the florist and the coupon? Which do you feel like more often: the crumpled up piece of paper or the flowers? Why? What was Angela's one fear? Have you ever felt that same fear? If so, how? What did Angela mean when she said that "all that really matters is the eye of the beholder"? How did Alyssa from BarlowGirl**

celebrate God's opinion of herself? Then say: **Today, we're going to try Alyssa's experiment.** Distribute a piece of paper and a pen to each girl and direct girls to go to different parts of the room for privacy. Direct girls to think about the last few weeks and what they've learned about God's opinion of them. Lead teens to list as many adjectives as they can think of to describe how God feels about them. However, when they write, girls should begin each statement by writing, "I am." They are to complete that statement by using words that describe God's view of them.

Call girls back together. Say: **In the DVD segment today, Alyssa said she felt a little arrogant for writing down God's view of her.** Ask: **Did you feel uncomfortable writing down statements affirming your worth? Why or why not?** Challenge girls to read aloud the sentences they created. You may need to get girls started by reading your own statements. Ask: **Was it difficult to read those statements aloud? Why or why not?** Then say: **Angela challenged us to celebrate the fact that God is wild about us. That's what we'll be doing today.**

Festive Surroundings (option)
If your meeting space will be conducive to decoration, take the time to make your surroundings festive. Hang decorative lights. Create a banner announcing, "Celebrate!" Get framed photos of girls from their par-

ents and display them around the room. Enlist some adults to supply snacks and drinks. Play some upbeat, Christian music. As girls arrive, encourage them to enjoy the festivities as they mingle and look at pictures. After all the girls have arrived, say: **You're all the guests of honor at this celebration. Today, we'll be celebrating the love God has for us.**

Looking Back

Direct girls to the Mall Maze quiz on pages 106-107. Say: **Nothing tests our understanding of God's love for us and our own worth more than a visit to the mall. While we're there, we're bombarded with thousands of messages that tell us how we're supposed to look, who we're supposed to be with, what we're supposed to wear. It can be overwhelming. This "trip" through the mall will help you test your growth over these last few weeks.** Challenge girls to complete the quiz honestly. After a few minutes, allow girls to share how they did. Say: **It's OK if you're still struggling. These truths take a lifetime to learn. However, even though we're still learning and growing in God's amazing love for us, we can still seek to celebrate our lives as God has created us.**

Living Lab (option)

If your group would enjoy a trip to the mall (as would most girls), you might want to make the above quiz come alive by taking the girls to a local shopping mall. Give each girl a small notebook and a pen. Pair girls into teams and assign a part of the mall to each team. Instruct them to walk through their segment of the shopping mall to identify and evaluate the messages they see and hear. Also encourage them to take note of how they felt as they noticed those messages. At a designated time and place, meet back together to talk about what the girls observed and felt. Debrief by asking questions such as: **Do you think you noticed more messages than in the past because of our study? Were you able to pinpoint which messages made you feel badly about yourself? Why or why not? How do you think you'll combat these messages the next time you're in the mall? How can you continue to live out over the next few weeks what you've learned?**

Time to Celebrate

Ask: **What are some things people celebrate?** Challenge girls to think of as many types of celebrations as they can. List these on a large sheet of paper if space allows. If girls need prompting, give them a few examples to start: birthday, anniversary, spiritual anniversary, retirement, winning a sporting event, completing a project. After girls have exhausted their lists, point out the fact that little attention was given to celebrating God's love. Ask: **Why do you think we as Christians don't celebrate God's love on a regular basis?** *(laziness, forgetfulness, disbelief, unconfessed sin, apathy, distractions, trials)* Say: **Let's look at a Scripture passage that will give us some hints about celebrating. As a group, read Psalm 149:1-5 together.** Challenge girls to read this passage with strong voices and emotion. Then direct girls to read this passage again, making note of each command to praise referenced *(sing, praise, rejoice, dance, make music)* Ask: **What reason is given for such celebration?** *(God takes delight in people and saves them, v. 4)* Say: **When you begin to understand and live in God's love, you will be changed emotionally, spiritually, mentally, socially—every aspect of your life. Let's see how that might look.**

Song Time (option)

If you have a particularly musical group of teen girls, you may want to work with them to create a song based on what they've learned over the last few weeks. They can use the tune of an existing song, or they can even create their own melody. If you choose to do the closing celebration (see pages 31-32), work with the girls to perform this song at that event. You may even want to work with the music minister at your church to allow the girls to sing the song as a part of an upcoming corporate worship service.

Well-rounded Person

Direct girls to the "My Way" sections on pages 115, 117, 119 and 121. Highlight the fact that these are different facets of their lives in which they can celebrate God's love in practical, tangible ways. Have a little fun working through these pages by doing a "lightning round." Give girls 30 seconds to complete "Physical Celebration" on pages 114-115. After 30 seconds, direct girls to turn the page and complete the next section. Repeat this process until each of the sections has been completed. Then direct girls to return to "Physical Celebration" and lead girls to share some of their answers. Repeat this process for the other sections. Encourage girls to write down answers they liked from others.

Closing Prayer Time

If you have a large meeting space, print on separate, large pieces of paper the statements from page 128 of the student book. Tape these statements around the room. Distribute markers and challenge girls to list their answers on each paper. Encourage them to list more than one answer per question. After several minutes, review each of the lists and call on girls to expound on their answers. Also be willing to share from your own experiences in this study. If you don't have adequate small space or have a small group of girls, direct them to go to the questions on page 128 and answer them in their books. Spark discussion as instructed above. Then say: **Today is the end of our study, but it's not the end of your growth and learning. To close our time together, I'd like for us to pray together.** Direct girls to review what they wrote down for the last response on page 128. Explain that during the prayer time, they will have the opportunity to pray what they've written. Play quiet praise music in the background, and open the prayer time by offering your own prayer to Jesus about how you feel about yourself. Your honesty will set the stage for this prayer time. After teens have prayed, close the time together by praying for each of the girls.

If you would like to celebrate this study in a more elaborate fashion, read "Closing Celebration" on the next two pages. This article contains ideas and suggestions for involving your church and the girls' families in celebrating God's amazing love for the girls.❀

Closing Celebration

To make this Bible study memorable to the girls in your student ministry, consider hosting a dinner celebration to end your time together. In this article, we've provided some suggestions for carrying out such an event. Your church may choose to add or change elements according to your ethnic, geographic, or economic makeup. You may not be able to do everything suggested, or you may be able to host an event more elaborate that the one described. That's OK. You know the needs and the resources of your students and your church. The goal is to provide a memorable experience for the girls, their families, and your church. The event should honor the girls and highlight the main principle of this book: that God is wild about them and that He pursues them with a life-changing, satisfying love that cannot be duplicated or substituted by anything else.

A Meal

Plan a meal for the girls, their families, friends, and the other significant adults in their lives (adult leaders, teachers, coaches, etc.). Long before the banquet, direct the girls to make a list of people they would like to invite. Put a limit on the number of guests if necessary, but make sure you don't exclude any immediate family members.

Plan a meal within your budgetary means. If you have the funds, cater the meal. If you are on a shoestring budget, ask church members to cook. Once you've explained the banquet and what you hope to accomplish, you'll have lots of cooks on your hands! The meal doesn't have to be complicated. The goal is to bring together the important people in each girl's life.

Special Speaker

During this celebration, invite a special guest to speak briefly. Direct your speaker to provide a closing charge based on the content of *Wild About You*. The person may want to recap some of the principles for the girls and to let guests know what the girls have been learning. He or she should encourage, inspire, and challenge the girls to live out the truths they have discovered.

The Blessing

The most significant aspect of this celebration is giving the blessing. During this special time, each girl should be recognized individually. The closest people in her life (friends, family, teachers) will have the opportunity to share the gifts, talents, and abilities they see in her. Encourage them to uplift the girl by talking about specific qualities—physical, emotional, spiritual, social, and cognitive. If possible, the last person to speak should be the girl's father. He should talk about his love and support of his daughter and the importance of living in the greater love of God. If a father cannot attend, ask the mother to speak. If neither parent is available, enlist the help of another significant adult (Sunday School teacher, brother, grandparent, etc.). Based on the number of girls in your group, you may want to limit the time each person speaks. If you have a large group, you may want to allow only the parents to speak. If the night drags on, it will lose its significance.

Because this is such an important element of the ceremony, contact the guests beforehand and challenge them to prepare a brief statement. Call them or e-mail them, or you may want to give the girls in your group the responsibility of telling their guests about the blessing. Be warned: girls who are not used to being in the spotlight may "forget" to tell others in hopes that she can remain in the shadows. You will want to make sure none of the girls gets left out.

Once the blessings have been pronounced on each girl, direct the guests to circle around the girl they have come to honor. Instruct guests to place a hand on the girl's head and to pray that God would allow the girl to live in the reality of God's amazing love for her, and that she would pursue and experience that love daily.

Presentation of a Gift

Another element to include in the celebration is a gift given by the parents (or other significant adult) to the girls. Once a father has spoken, he should give his daughter a special gift by which to remember the celebration and Bible study. The gift can be as elaborate as a bracelet or as simple but important as a family heirloom. Challenge the fathers to think of something unique to his daughter's personality and reflective of his dreams and desires for her as a godly woman. The father (or mother) should explain the meaning behind the item chosen.

You may need to advise parents against buying elaborate gifts that may make some of the other girls feel uncomfortable or embarrassed about their own financial status. The goal is not to use money to communicate love, worth, or status, but rather to provide something tangible and meaningful by which to mark the occasion.

Other Issues to Consider

Invitations and Decorations. Prior to the celebration, send out invitations. Allow girls in your group to create the invitations on a computer or from scratch. Local craft stories carry invitation kits. Send out the invitations at least three weeks in advance, and instruct your guests to RSVP so that you can plan the meal accordingly.

Decorations can be as simple or elaborate as the invitations. String special lights (white Christmas lights work great), create centerpieces for each table, and use special serving dishes or silverware. If possible, enlist the help of some creative people in your church who excel in decorating.

Slide Show. As a part of the celebration, you may want to prepare a slide show of the girls. Gather pictures of the girls at various ages, beginning with infancy and concluding in the present. If you have taken pictures of the girls throughout the six weeks of study, include those as well. Include music in the background as the presentation runs. (You might want to feature music by BarlowGirl since their interviews are featured in the study.)

Testimonies. If any of your students are willing, enlist one or two of them to give testimonies about what this study has meant to them. Encourage them to review the past quizzes, articles, and other features of the magazine to help them put into words the things they have learned. You may also want to share a few words with the audience about what God has taught you through the experience.

DVD Sampling. As adults, parents, and teens are arriving for the celebration, play parts of the DVD segments. You may want to start the DVD at the first session and let it play through all segments, or you may want to choose some of the teens' most memorable segments and play those. It will give the guests a small taste of the experiences teens shared together. ✿